C000212618

ANNIVER
CLOCKS

Peter Wotton

SHIRE PUBLICATIONS

First published in Great Britain in 2009 by Shire
Publications Ltd, Midland House, West Way, Botley,
Oxford OX2 0PH, United Kingdom.
443 Park Avenue South, New York, NY 10016, USA.

E-mail: shire@shirebooks.co.uk   www.shirebooks.co.uk

A CIP catalogue record for this book is available from the
British Library.

Shire Library no. 331   •   ISBN-13: 978 0 7478 0733 9

Peter Wotton has asserted his right under the Copyright,
Designs and Patents Act, 1988, to be identified as the
author of this book.

Designed by Ken Vail Graphic Design, Cambridge, UK and
typeset in Perpetua and Gill Sans.
Printed in Malta by Gutenberg Press Ltd.

09 10 11 12 13   10 9 8 7 6 5 4 3 2 1

COVER IMAGE
A rare, heavily ornate ormolu – in this case, gold-plated
brass – example (c. 1951) by Kern and Sohne. This
company was the direct descendant of Kienzle.

TITLE PAGE IMAGE
1930s Mahogany case example by Kundo with a
pendulum following the Kienzle style.

ACKNOWLEDGEMENTS

For those who unknowingly contributed to this
monograph; particular thanks are due to the late Jon Hoff.
An exceptionally gifted artist, horologist and friend of
many years, this small volume owes much to Jon's sharing
of his wide professional knowledge and experience.
Specific recognition is also due to the late Charles
Terwilliger, author of the *400-day Clock Repair Guide*.

Shire Publications is supporting the Woodland Trust, the UK's leading woodland conservation charity, by funding the dedication of trees.

CONTENTS

INTRODUCTION

THE MEASUREMENT of time stretches back as far as history. Time has been measured by the sun, moon and stars, by the flow of water, sand and pebbles, and by the burning of a flame. Such methods have appeared in some form or other in every important civilisation. Mechanical devices for measuring time, however, have a shorter history. But as early as 1288, a crude mechanical clock, Great Tom, was built at Westminster.

In 1657 Christiaan Huygens, a Dutchman, patented the gravity pendulum clock. This pendulum is the one commonly seen in a grandfather clock, where a weight swings from side to side under the influence of gravity. It was the first working mechanism for the accurate measurement of small time intervals, and its scientific importance was enormous. The seventeenth century ended in a flurry of activity and invention, which secured the dominance of the mechanical clock.

Right: An excellent example of a high-quality, rectangular-faced anniversary clock by Gustav Becker, c. 1905.

Far right: Anniversary clock by Phillipp Haas, c. 1905, using four pillars.

There had been automata clocks with moving figures as early as the mid sixteenth century, and from that point onwards, interest in clocks that did more than tell the time gradually expanded. During Victorian times a large market for inexpensive novelty clocks developed. Commercially, the anniversary clock originated as a Black Forest novelty clock. It offered a unique and fascinating pendulum display and required winding only once a year because the pendulum moved so slowly – about thirty times more slowly than a typical 'marble' clock of the period, which was wound weekly. As these clocks would run for over a year on one winding, this feature was linked to the idea that they should only be wound on the anniversary of some special event. The name 'Anniversary' was registered as a trademark in 1901 by Bowler and Burdick, a retailer from Cleveland, Ohio, USA. The idea had instant appeal and the name stuck. The clocks became classic anniversary presents, and their owners commonly attached strong sentimental value to them.

Above: Another anniversary clock by Haas, c. 1905.

The anniversary clock is a simple mechanical timepiece (a clock without a strike) and may be considered as being made up of four components: the movement, pendulum assembly, casework and display front.

Throughout this book, the emphasis is on clocks still generally obtainable on the antique market. Apart from specific definitions, which are explained in the text, the terminology used is in accordance with de Carle's *Watch and Clock Encyclopaedia* (*see* Further Reading).

Far left: A rare example of a Junghans anniversary clock, produced in c. 1910, a time when disc pendulums were being overtaken in popularity by ball pendulums.

Left: This late example by Jfk (c. 1950) was advertised as a 1,000-day clock. Jfk also made a similar 500-day version.

THE FIRST MAKERS

This illustration is of a classical four-glass clock case usually seen with a normal gravity pendulum. Suppliers bought their cases and movements separately and fitted them together according to current trends – in this case with an anniversary clock movement. This is an early model (c.1900) with the movement fixed to the top of the case. Note the seven-pillar screwed-gallery pendulum with hook attachment; the maker is Becker, who copied Jfk closely.

HUYGENS had experimented with the torsion pendulum (in which a weighted disc rotates around a vertical wire – called a suspension spring – twisting it, instead of swinging from side to side like an ordinary pendulum) in the seventeenth century, but his experiments never came to fruition. In the years that followed, a number of patents were taken out for torsion pendulum clocks by Leslie (Great Britain, 1793), Crane (USA, 1841), Terry (USA, 1852), Hile (USA, 1876), Jehlin (Germany, 1879 – the patent passing to Harder on Jehlin's death) and Harder (Germany, 1880, and USA, 1882). Crane and Terry both produced working clocks and a number are still extant, such as the weight-driven, three-ball pendulum example (1842) by Crane, now displayed in the New Jersey State Museum. For the most part, however, these patents had little or no impact on the commercial market; Harder was to become the exception.

In 1879 Harder made the first attempt to progress his invention through A. Willman & Company. Willman, founded in 1872, operated in the Silesian area of Germany close to the Polish border, primarily making regulator wall clocks.

Willman was a small, struggling company with few marketing skills, and it faced a loss of consumer confidence due to the failure and poor timekeeping of many of its models. (Many working clocks were made and sold with verge, cylinder and Graham escapements, but none of the designs was wholly successful.) The prohibitive expense of finding a complete answer to its problems that would win back a now prejudiced customer led to the company seeking support elsewhere.

By 1880 Willman was almost certain to have undertaken sub-contract work for the giant Becker Company, and there existed a respectful relationship between the two companies. Becker's involvement in developing the 400-day clock was initiated by Willman, and this included the sharing of background information.

Gustav Becker (1819–85) started his company in 1847 from the humblest of beginnings. Some thirty years later, at the birth of the 400-day clock, he was on the Royal Crown Trade Commission and an internationally recognised figure at the peak of his career. By 1880, however, Becker himself was already ailing, and Harder, like any individualistic inventor, would have been somewhat smothered by a large, impersonal firm. Becker's attempts to find a quick, simple solution to the reliability issue failed, and Harder was compelled to review his position, making parallel arrangements with another small company, the Fortuna Clock Company from Triberg in the Black Forest; unfortunately the clock continued to be unreliable.

In 1880, after buying some equipment from the estate of the deceased Michael Bob, August Schatz set up a workshop and initially continued to produce Bob's range of clocks. At this time Schatz was in partnership with Gerson Wintermantel, and the firm was initially known as Wintermantel and Co. The logo of a 'W' inside half an escape wheel is that of the Wintermantel Brothers (Otto and Eugen), founded in 1924 by Albert Wintermantel, whose name is also to be seen on early 400-day clocks.

THE GREATEST OF ALL GREAT BARGAINS
and the
GREATEST OF ALL ADVERTISING OFFERS

THIS WONDERFUL CLOCK GOES FOR 400 DAYS WITH ONE WINDING

The Clock for Kitchen Bedroom or Drawing Room. The Clock for Attractiveness and Usefulness. The most handsome and Reliable Clock ever invented. Every Clock is warranted for 10 years and guaranteed to keep accurate time for over a year with ONE ordinary winding.

Sent on First Payment

of **2/-** only.

Balance 2/- Monthly. After you have received the Clock

For a short period only we are offering a limited number of these valuable Patent Clocks (of which the usual price is two guineas) for 20/- each only, and, as a huge advertisement and in order to enable everyone to come into possession of these magnificent timekeepers, the British Clothing Club (Jewellery Dept.), 74, Oldham Street, Manchester, will send them safely packed in a strong box free, to any address, on receipt of first payment of 2/- only, to all approved orders. The balance (18/-) to be paid at 2/- per month after you have received and examined the goods, and if perfectly satisfied. These clocks are polished brass finish throughout, and of first-class quality and workmanship (size 1ft by 8in.). A clock for every home; a clock for a lifetime. Send 2/- Deposit at once to secure this wonderful bargain. Money returned in full if not entirely satisfied. Customers are offered a splendid present as cash bonus if the full amount is remitted.

Cross your postal order and keep the Counterfoil and this advert. for reference.

"A Thing of Beauty and a Joy for Ever."

Don't Miss This Opportunity of a Lifetime.

This advertisement will not appear every day

An early paper advertisement for a Becker anniversary clock, c. 1905. Although not too clear in the paper's illustration, the pendulum is of the seven-pillar screwed-gallery variety. The clock is being promoted here by the British Clothing Club (Jewellery Department).

Right: This Jfk clock, the third generation, still has the square pillar base washers, but the dial is slightly larger, with an ornate surround and spade-style hands. Note also the high quality, heavy manufacture throughout the whole clock.

Below: This anniversary clock example comes from Jfk's first production line. Compared with the standard models, the points to note are: its lower height due to the lack of any pendulum gallery; pinned attachment between the pendulum and suspension spring; the square pillar base washers; and a dial which is of smaller diameter than the plate width.

It would appear that Harder met Schatz some time after arrangements had been made with Fortuna. Schatz – whose business acumen is confirmed by the future success of Jfk – suggested improvements to facilitate manufacture of the 400-day clock. Still frustrated by his experience with Willman, Harder was easily diverted to the possibility of a new company dedicated solely to his own invention. At any event, in 1881 Harder, under Schatz's leadership, became part of a newly formed company, Jahresuhren-fabrik (Jfk). The company operated from Triberg and almost certainly included ex-employees from Fortuna. After 1945 the company name became Schatz to celebrate its founder.

The first production of anniversary clocks was in March 1882. In December of the same year Harder repeated his patent in the USA. He sold his rights to deGruyter of Amsterdam in 1884, and the patent was allowed to lapse in 1887. Competition truly started in 1888, when Lenzkirche Uhrenfabrik (at Lenzkirche in Germany) entered the market. Lenzkirche amalgamated with Junghans in 1927. No clocks from Lenzkirche appear to have been identified, and it is possible that they marketed clocks made by Becker, with whom despite their wide geographical separation – they had a close relationship (including some joint advertising). Badische Uhrenfabrik entered the field in 1889; this important and highly individualistic company became one of the top producers of anniversary clocks. With one exception (Claude Grivolas, France, 1908), early competition was solely from German companies. Japan did not enter the market until after 1945.

The name '400-day clock' (plus the striking deGruyter patent) first appeared in 1885, on the dials of striking anniversary clocks made by Jfk. Examples from this period have appeared with the word 'Anniversary' marked on both the back plate and the dial. Although offered by a number of manufacturers over the years, striking anniversary clocks were a failure: they were highly expensive, kept poor time and had insufficient power for the strike mechanism.

In 1898 Willman, together with the plethora of companies that grew up around Becker, were involved in negotiations that resulted in their amalgamation under the company name 'United Freiburg Clock Factories A. G. Formerly Gustav Becker' (contemporary British retailers sometimes referred to this group as 'USC'). In 1926 the group merged with Junghans.

Junghans patented a pendulum-regulating device in 1884. The same year also marks the start of the Thomas Haller factory at Schwenningen, which merged with Junghans in 1900; this company is credited with a 400-day clock, centred on the escapement and patented in 1882–3.

Schatz's major contribution was the emphasis on a Graham escapement. Together with the method of adjustment, this led to stability in escapement operation. Becker, who initially used a cylinder escapement (and who also used a verge escapement along the lines of the original Jehlin patent), rapidly converted to an adjustable Graham escapement using Harder's design, patented in America in 1882.

Prior to 1888, Becker and Jfk were, commercially, the dominant companies, with mechanisms almost identical in style and construction. Badische Uhrenfabrik entered the market in 1888, and rapidly achieved a comparable commercial status. Badische also had a special relationship with a Dr Kienzle, whose company produced a number of innovative pendulums and suspension brackets – the company name, Kienzle Clock Factories, started to appear about this time as he took over the family concern. Badische used pendulums made by Kienzle, while Kienzle used movements made by Badische. Badische operated from Furtwangen and was the 1889 amalgamation of two geographically close Black Forest companies: Leo Faller from Guttenbach, and Uhrenfabrik Furtwangen from Furtwangen. These firms, situated roughly halfway between Lenzkirch Uhrenfabrik and Jfk, were equipped for producing American-style mass-produced movements for the 'popular' end of the market.

From their beginnings in 1889, the Badische Company grew rapidly, peaking commercially during the first few years of the twentieth century. Unlike many other companies they did not re-open properly in 1918. While they did continue in existence, their manufacturing interest in the 400-day market declined – though a few of their original models may have been produced in small batches. In 1923 they were apparently stagnant, picking up after 1927 and again after 1932. Dismantled after 1945, the company was then revived and added a branch at Simonswald. Between about 1953 and 1955 they were responsible for a few 400-day patents, notably the Kaiser rotating world pendulum. In 1979 Badische are quoted as having 180 employees, but in the 1980s they faced decline once more, coming to an end at about the same time as Schatz (Jfk), in 1985.

This Tiffany Never-Wind electric clock belongs to the first few years of the twentieth century. One of the earliest electric clocks, it was particularly successful on the American market at a time when the mechanical anniversary clock had become popular.

Around 1954 two novel forms of the anniversary clock were produced by Uhrenfabrik J. Kaiser to a Badische patent (approved in 1955). The best-known Kaiser World Clock (shown *left*) is relatively complicated compared to a normal anniversary clock and has an active moon phase indicator. Kaiser's second World Clock (*right*) is more rare and follows an Art Nouveau styling with a more detailed world, but it lacks a moon phase.

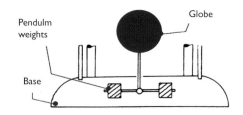

Pendulm weights

Base

Globe

Middle: the normal style pendulum weight system, hidden inside the base. Weight adjustment is via the knurled disc above each world.

Right: detail of the worlds used on the Kaiser World Clocks.

MOVEMENT

A NNIVERSARY CLOCK mechanisms are generally considered to be in four sizes, based on the size of the plates: standard (65 × 85 mm), used from 1882 to the early 1960s; narrow standard (40 × 85 mm), from 1951; miniature (45 × 62 mm), from *c*. 1950; and midget (45 × 52 mm), from *c*. 1957. There are many small variations, particularly in the miniature and midget sizes.

The anniversary clock movement (or mechanism) consists of four parts: the power source, the gear train, the escapement and the motion work. The illustrations in this chapter show a typical anniversary clock movement with transparent rear plate so that the mechanism can be clearly viewed.

POWER SOURCE

In the purely mechanical anniversary clock, the power is produced by a mainspring. A wound mainspring represents a large force that operates over a small distance. Winding a 400-day anniversary clock from relaxed to fully wound, for example, is achieved in five turns of the key.

GEAR TRAIN

The gear train translates the output of the power source into a small force operating over a large distance. Two types of gear train were initially used: Badische clocks have six wheels (W1, W2, W3, CW (Centre Wheel), W4 and EW (Escape Wheel)); Jfk and other companies have five wheels (lacking W4). In both cases the true fourth wheel was known as the centre wheel, with the last wheel in the train being the escape wheel. The difference between the two types is not concerned with the total gear ratio but the number of teeth per wheel.

This example shows the mainspring barrel (power unit) connected to the first wheel only.

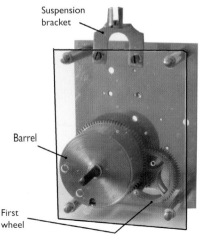

Suspension bracket

Barrel

First wheel

Power is the rate of work per second; work is the force available multiplied by the distance travelled. The total amount of work, originated by the mainspring, is clearly the same from first wheel to escape wheel (apart from losses such as friction), but the distance moved by the escape wheel is amplified by the gear ratio. Hence, only a small force is available at the escape wheel, which will rotate over 20,000 times for every full turn of the winding key.

Another aspect that distinguishes Badische wheels from those of other manufacturers is their use of lantern pinions. These consist of rods clamped between two discs (rather like a disc pendulum's pillar system). Badische was equipped with up-to-date mass production machinery from their start, and economic manufacture was a critical part of their success – to which they added considerable innovative skill (they produced a huge range of popular-priced clocks). Lantern pinion production could be automated on their machinery, and pinions were less expensive to produce in this form. Such pinions are easier to repair than solid pinions.

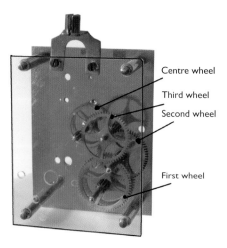

Centre wheel

Third wheel

Second wheel

First wheel

Above: This example shows the first, second, third and centre wheels only. With slight differences in position and numbers of wheel teeth this construction was standard for all early companies except Badische.

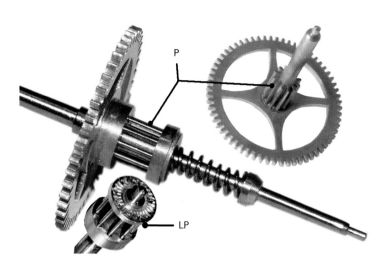

P

LP

Above: This illustration (Badische, c. 1910) demonstrates two features: the use of a centre-wheel shaft that is spring held to the centre wheel for adjustment of the hands; and a comparison between lantern pinions (P *left*) and solid pinions (P *right*). A portion showing a lantern pinion at a different angle (LP) is shown just below the main picture.

ESCAPEMENT

In a grandfather clock, power is transferred from the escapement to a pendulum rod via a rigid link. In the anniversary clock (where the force of gravity is replaced by the stress generated in the suspension spring), the pendulum rod is a flexible wire strip. Power is now transferred from the mechanism to this suspension spring strip via the fork. ('Fluttering' – unwanted vibration – of the fork is easily produced and the escape wheel then shoots through an indeterminate number of teeth, ruining the timekeeping.)

In principle there are many different escapement types that could be used. It was Schatz's contribution to find an escapement and a method of adjustment that overcame the early problems. All the early anniversary clocks used a Graham escapement with a pin in the anchor, through which power was transferred to the fork. Later, Badische successfully used a pin-pallet escapement (as used on cheaper pocket watches). The speed of the escape wheel decides the speed of every other gear in the mechanism. The anchor controls movement of the teeth of the escape wheel. Teeth are released, or 'escape', one tooth at a time. Movement of the anchor pin

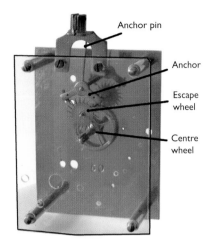

Anchor pin
Anchor
Escape wheel
Centre wheel

Above: This example shows the centre wheel, escape wheel and anchor. The escape wheel and anchor are together known as the 'escapement'.

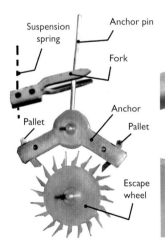

Suspension spring
Anchor pin
Fork
Pallet
Anchor
Pallet
Escape wheel

Escape wheel
Pin pallet

Far left: In this enlarged illustration of the escapement assembly, with a Graham escapement, the fork has been moved around 90 degrees anti-clockwise (viewed from above) for clarity. Note also that in this example the pallets' positions are adjustable.

Above right: An enlarged illustration of a pin-pallet escapement assembly by Badische (c.1910). This type of escapement may be found in many mass-produced, low-priced mantel clocks of the early twentieth century. Properly made, this escapement can give excellent results. Apart from Badische it was not used in anniversary clocks until the mid 1950s. The only problem with the escapement is its lightweight construction and the difficulty of avoiding 'flutter' during adjustment.

– and the anchor itself – is controlled by the pendulum. As a tooth escapes, power from the mainspring is passed back through the anchor pin/fork connection via the suspension spring to the pendulum, making up for any losses, such as friction, in the process.

MOTION WORK

The motion work consists of a three-wheel train: the cannon pinion, the minute wheel and the hour wheel. These wheels are 'tapped' into the main gear train with the sole purpose of translating the movement of the gear train into a visual display of time on a dial. The cannon pinion (to which the minute hand is attached) is either spring or friction tight to the centre wheel shaft and drives the minute wheel. The minute wheel drives the hour wheel to which the hour hand is attached. The minute hand may be adjusted manually without affecting the main gear train because of the spring/friction-fit between the cannon pinion and the centre wheel shaft.

Although the minute hand of an anniversary clock is normally a push-fit on the cannon pinion, Badische have a slightly different approach (as used, for example, on some Garrard clocks). The centre-wheel shaft is spring held to the centre wheel. The minute hand, fixed to a squared, extended centre-wheel shaft, can therefore be freely turned to correct the time without influencing the main movement (*see* p. 12).

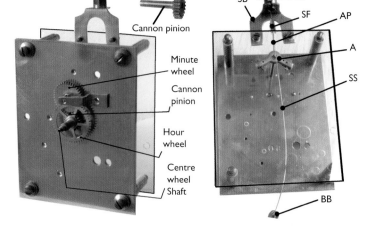

Right: This example shows the motion work situated at the front of the movement behind the dial. The hidden cannon pinion is also shown separately (*top right*).

Cannon pinion

Minute wheel

Cannon pinion

Hour wheel

Centre wheel
Shaft

SB — TB
SF — AP
A
SS
BB

Above right: This example shows: the suspension bracket (SB); the anchor (A) and anchor pin (AP, behind the suspension spring); the suspension spring (SS) hanging on the suspension bracket via the top block (TB); and the engagement between the suspension spring fork (SF) and the anchor pin. The bottom block (BB) is connected to the pendulum.

PENDULUM ASSEMBLY

THE FULL pendulum assembly consists of three components: the pendulum itself; the suspension spring (with its attached fork, upper and lower blocks); and the suspension bracket (concerned with the critical in-beat adjustments).

THE PENDULUM

The first pendulums were discs machined out of a solid cylinder of brass. Two small adjustable weights were provided on top of the disc for altering the number of pendulum rotations per minute. The weights were connected by means of a rod with opposite-handed screw threads at each end. Turning the rod from either end moved both of the discs inwards or outwards. Each end

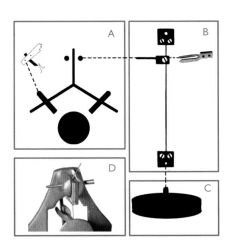

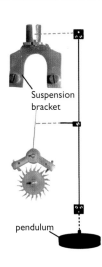

Suspension bracket

pendulum

Far left: In this diagrammatic representation of the pendulum assembly the movement's escapement (A) connects (dotted line) to the suspension spring assembly (B) via a fork. The bottom block of the suspension spring (B) holds the pendulum (C); the top block of the suspension spring suspends the whole assembly on a suspension bracket (D).

Above right: The pendulum assembly, shown here, consists of the escapement assembly, the pendulum, the suspension spring, and the suspension bracket. The escapement assembly consists of an escape wheel and anchor. Power, originating at the mainspring, is transferred to the escapement assembly's anchor pin, then to the suspension spring via the fork, and finally to the rotating pendulum where it compensates for losses.

Right: Jfk's first pendulum is here shown with the adjustable weights separated. Note also the clock key – one end for winding the clock and the other for adjusting the square at the end of the weights' rod.

Far right: The earliest disc pendulums were pinned to the bottom block of the suspension spring. Pinning (left) only appears on Jfk pendulums. The change to hook attachment (right) first appears on later Jfk six-pillar screwed-gallery pendulums.

Right: This temperature-compensating pendulum (c.1894) follows the same bi-metallic arm principle used for watch balances. This was the earliest attempt to solve the temperature problem and was produced by Phillipp Haas (Hauck) according to the French patent by J. J. Meister, 1892. This is an early example without a gallery.

of the rod was squared for key use, and anniversary clocks with disc pendulums were therefore, like carriage clocks, provided with double-ended keys.

Pendulums hang on a small block, which is clamped to the bottom end of the suspension spring. Originally the block was pinned directly onto the pendulum, but after 1898 a hook attachment was generally used, making disconnection easier.

During the troublesome developmental period of 1879–82, discs of 10 cm diameter were tried. In 1880 an experimental clock by Gustav Becker used a 9.2 cm diameter pendulum weighing 330 grams. The first commercially successful batch of anniversary clocks from Jfk was delivered in March 1882. These clocks were regulated by a disc pendulum, and the original examples were 9 cm in diameter and weighed 300 grams. By 1883 the discs were reduced to 8.5 cm in diameter, weighing 250 grams. Timekeeping accuracy was still appalling, however, being affected by the smallest change of temperature.

The first change to the disc pendulum was the addition of a gallery mounted above the disc (the gallery is purely ornamental). A gallery consists of a number of vertically mounted pillars held between two plates; the side screws hold the pillars to the plates. The first galleries used three pillars and were introduced by Jfk in 1885.

It was initially assumed that the poor timekeeping was caused by temperature-controlled variations in the length of the suspension spring. In 1892, Meister of France patented a compensating pendulum for the anniversary clock. His solution was based on a pendulum disc made from strips of brass and steel, which expanded at different rates, thus altering the disc diameter according to temperature. Prototype drawings show a pendulum similar in appearance to a compensated watch balance wheel. This pendulum has appeared on the antique market but is very rare. The patent was developed by Hauck (Haas) of Munich, and his version appeared on the market in 1894. Initially it was without any gallery (hook attachment) but appeared later with a small diameter gallery of a form that is particular to Phillipp Haas. The pendulum failed to compensate for the effect of temperature changes and had a short market life.

From 1902 to 1903 a further series of temperature-compensating disc pendulums was made: Huber's 1902 twin loop pendulum (one loop was used for compensation), seen on clocks by Jfk, Badische and Haas; Wille's 1902 design, using temperature variations of a threaded arm, seen on Jfk clocks; and the Kienzle version (c.1903), which used crossed mercury tubes for temperature compensation. The Kienzle pendulum (8.7 cm in diameter, weight 356 grams) is often wrongly allocated to Becker who also produced a range of compensating pendulums. All these pendulums are rare, highly ornamental and now much sought after. As with the Hauck (Haas) pendulum, they all aimed to compensate for alterations in the length of the suspension spring with changes in temperature. In fact they were compensating for an effect that was secondary. None of these methods tackled the real problem (the 'modulus of elasticity', explained below, p. 22) and all had a short commercial life.

With the exception of the French maker, Claude Grivolas (whose movement plates were circular), all manufacturers to the original standard plate size were German. Grivolas took out patents from about 1907 to 1910 in the UK and elsewhere. Although not usually included in the temperature-compensating group, a Grivolas catalogue does include the use of Invar (a nickel iron alloy). Invar and Elinvar are nickel-chrome alloys. Invar (INVARiable) has a low temperature coefficient of expansion/contraction – used for pendulum rods. Elinvar (ELasticity INVARiable) retains a constant elasticity with temperature – used for watch balance springs and anniversary clock suspension springs. It seems quite likely that Grivolas experimented with Elinvar, while the special suspension spring (in two halves – shown in the illustrations) on one of his clocks does indicate a close interest and awareness of temperature compensation.

Below far left: This is a later example of the Haas temperature-compensated disc pendulum (c.1894) and has their distinctive, smaller diameter five-pillar top-screwed gallery.

Left: Between c.1902 and 1906, a range of special compensating pendulums was produced, attempting (unsuccessfully) to compensate for alterations in suspension spring length with changes of temperature. This example by Kienzle (c.1905) is typical, and its rarity attracts a high price.

Top left: A Phillip Haas pendulum (c.1908). By this time the disc pendulum had become obsolete, replaced by the ball pendulum. This example, for a Haas 'Semester' (six months) anniversary clock, obviously seeks to attract interest from both pendulum persuasions. The balls move via a strip, and adjustment is made by sliding the balls into position and then clamping with a top screw (missing). The two 'A's stand for *Avance* (*Retard* appears on the other side).

Top middle: A Jfk six-pillar top-screwed gallery pendulum. In this design a single rod, extending from the suspension spring's hook attachment point to the disc base, holds the pillar plate assembly together. In the less common example shown, a top twist has been added. This allowed the same suspension spring length to be used with differing case heights.

Top right: This illustration shows the first Jfk six-pillar screwed-gallery pendulum with pin attachment for the suspension spring; hook attachment appears with later examples of this pendulum. Note the lack of any central pillar.

The first galleried pendulums with six pillars began to appear just before 1900 – the six-pillar screwed-gallery pendulum. The style originated with Jfk but was rapidly copied by Becker. These early, heavy-looking examples used screws in the upper and lower plates of the gallery to hold the pillars in position. They are both approximately 8.5 cm in diameter with a weight of 400 grams. The distinguishing feature, immediately recognisable, of Becker's pendulums is the larger diameter of the lower plate holding the pillars. Becker also used a seventh, shaped central pillar, which is easily missed – the seven-pillar screwed-gallery pendulum. This screwed method of holding the upper and lower plates of the gallery has a visual charm, but it is component and labour intensive. It was soon replaced by a central screwed rod, which with many small variations became the standard for future disc pendulums – the screwed-rod pendulum. In this arrangement, a rod extends from the suspension spring hook attachment

Left: The seven-pillar screwed-gallery pendulum by Gustav Becker. Note the central pillar, the larger diameter lower pillar plate, and the hook attachment.

Far left: Becker followed Jfk's new design with their own six-pillar screwed-rod disc pendulum.

point and through the gallery plates (clamping the pillars between them), finally screwing into the top of the pendulum's disc. A diameter of 8.5 cm and a total weight of 360 grams would be fairly typical. At much the same time the narrow five-pillar screwed-rod gallery was added to the Haas compensating pendulum.

The anniversary clocks of Claude Grivolas, the only French manufacturer, are instantly recognisable by their movements and by their pendulums, in which the adjustable weights are held within the pendulum's casing.

For the most reliable escapement operation the weight of the pendulum should be concentrated at its periphery. In 1900 the first commercially effective ball pendulums, which were initially thought to be more attractive,

Far left: Early Badische clocks were issued with a standard six-pillar screwed-rod disc pendulum. Some, like the one shown, were made by Kienzle. Note that the 'gallery' is formed by stamping out the pillar shape from a flat sheet of brass and then bending the sheet round into standard gallery form.

Left: A complete breakdown of the previous Kienzle screwed-rod disc pendulum; note the rings for adjusting the disc's weight.

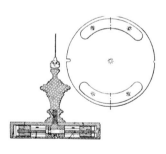

Above left: This illustration shows a breakdown of the Grivolas pendulum. Note the static lead weights (1), which may be changed by unscrewing their clamps; the square, key-adjustable weights (2, enlarged top left) travelling between the fixed lead weights; the side entry point for the key (3) in the disc cylinder; and the plate fixing and sealing the base of the disc (4).

Above right: This diagrammatic representation of the Grivolas disc pendulum shows the internal weights system.

Right: This Kienzle example (c.1902), with fancy side-screwed arms, is not often seen. There is no technical virtue in its unusual shape, but its rarity encourages a high price.

Middle and far right: The first four-ball pendulum came from Badische at the end of the nineteenth century. Jfk quickly followed (c.1905) with a better-designed version. The example in the middle is by Jfk and remained in the same form for the life of the anniversary clocks with standard-size movement plates (up to c.1950). The example to the right was issued in 1954 by Jfk under their new name, Schatz.

were marketed by Badische. In these the weight is almost totally concentrated at the periphery, making adjustment much easier. By 1914 disc pendulums had almost disappeared from the market.

Badische's first ball pendulum had four balls and was not adjustable. To allow correction for fast and slow, an adjustable bottom block or suspension bracket was provided, which effectively varied the length of the suspension spring. In 1902 Badische introduced the first adjustable three-ball pendulums (there are actually five balls but only three are adjustable). Altering the ball spacing was via the large milled disc at the top of the pendulum, a double key no longer being necessary. This, in a slightly altered form (with a central adjustment disc), became their standard ball pendulum; they also used a number of pendulums made by Kienzle, for whom they made movements.

Bottom left: This three-ball pendulum by Haas, c. 1905, is frequently seen. The difference in adjustment (by raising the top arm) is immediately apparent.

Bottom middle: This three-ball pendulum from Badische was the final version of their ball pendulum and the one most commonly available with their clocks. The milled adjustment disc is situated halfway up the pendulum.

Bottom right: This free-arm, four-ball example by Kienzle was produced c. 1908, about three years after Jfk's clamped-arm, four-ball design. A slightly different mechanism was used, distinguishable from the Jfk pendulum by the freer, more open ball display.

Far left: In c. 1908, Becker produced a free-arm, four-ball pendulum following the Kienzle style; this was the only ball pendulum example they produced.

Left: Jfk produced a number of variants based on their clamped-arm, four-ball design. This version (c.1906) is rare and strikingly different. Adjustment of the milled top disc moves the balls via a slit at the bottom of each arm.

Before 1914, four-ball pendulums developed along two specific lines. The first originated with Jfk in about 1905, and the style was followed in the years to come by companies such as Koma, Wurthner and Herr – the clamped-arm four-ball pendulum. Then, about 1908, came the Kienzle design whose style, based on the first Badische four-ball pendulum, was followed by Kundo, Henn, Kern (Kienzle's successor), Jauch and Haller and others – the free-arm four-ball pendulum.

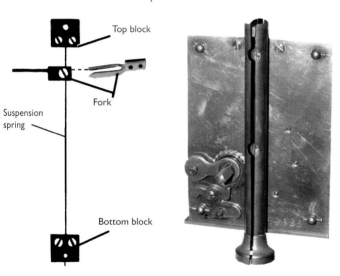

Top block

Fork

Suspension spring

Bottom block

Above left: This illustration of the suspension spring assembly consists of a bottom block for attaching to the pendulum, a fork for transferring power from the anchor pin, and a top block, which holds the top of the suspension spring to a suspension bracket.

Above right: The first suspension spring guard, the brass tube illustrated, was by Jfk (1905), and it is also seen on Kundo and Junghans anniversary clocks. The guard is screwed to the back plate and has a lengthwise split to allow changing of the suspension spring without removing the tube.

THE SUSPENSION SPRING

The pendulum was originally hung on a steel suspension spring. The timekeeping accuracy of anniversary clocks during this period was grossly affected by the smallest change in temperature. In addition, many clocks kept stopping for no apparent reason.

The pendulum assembly is delicate, the suspension spring in particular. In 1905 Jfk added a suspension spring guard, which not only protected the suspension spring, but also prevented the pendulum swinging and breaking the glass dome. The idea, in various forms, was rapidly copied by every other major manufacturer except Badische. Guards were fastened to the back plate. The main types were manufactured by Jfk, who used a tube with a belled end complete with a loose holding cup (rarely seen); Becker, who used a flat strip raised off the back plate, designated a 'safety bridge'; and Kienzle, who used two rings screwed to the back plate.

The suspension spring of 1882 was a steel strip. In 1904, C. Guillaume of France patented a nickel-chromium steel alloy, known as Elinvar, which offered a constant stiffness in the metal (modulus of elasticity). This could have provided a solution to the problem of temperature differences affecting timekeeping, but no manufacturer of anniversary clocks was interested. Around 1930, manufacturers introduced suspension springs made of bronze. These were cheaper to produce but were even more affected by temperature than steel. Despite this, within a short while they became standard. In 1949, when production of anniversary clocks was resumed after World War II, bronze suspension springs were still the norm.

Incredibly, over fifty years after the first introduction of the clock, timekeeping was still appalling. After 1945, under the instigation of the

Below right: The Becker suspension spring guard ('safety bridge') quickly followed after the Jfk guard in 1906, being a brass strip held from the back panel with four pillars. The top block (TB), suspension bracket (SB), suspension spring guard (SSG) and bottom block (BB) are identified on the illustration. Note the clamping arm (CA), which can be adjusted down onto the bottom block for clamping during movement or travelling.

Far right: Kienzle added two guard-rings within which the suspension spring twisted. In the illustration, the bottom block is missing and the suspension spring is only contained within the top guard-ring. The top and bottom blocks will not usually pass through the guard-rings without complete suspension spring disassembly; guard-rings are therefore often left off and lost after any repair work.

TB
SB
SSG
CA
BB

American Charles Terwilliger (*see* Further Reading), the US National Bureau of Standards was able to resolve the problem. They discovered that temperature changes resulted in a variation in stiffness of the suspension spring: changes in its length due to temperature were secondary. The Bureau recommended the use of either Elinvar or Ni Span 'C' (a patented nickel-chromium steel alloy similar to Elinvar). In 1951, Terwilliger had suspension springs made up from Ni Span 'C' and marketed them through his newly formed company, Horolovar. With these, an accuracy of plus or minus two minutes a week was easily attainable and they quickly became standard. As an example, a carefully set up anniversary clock using a Horolovar spring could run for six months without any need to re-adjust the time.

THE SUSPENSION BRACKET

The top of the suspension spring has to be reliably clamped in such a way that will take the full weight of the pendulum and the twisting suspension spring. One method would be to simply jam the strip spring into a slot. This would be very crude, though it was tried by Becker in their first clocks as well as by Vosseler on their 30-day lunar clocks (*c*.1910). A number of problems arose: for example, the only practical way to finely rotate the suspension spring (setting in beat) was to put a twist in it. In addition, due to variations in the level setting of the base of the clock, the suspension spring would be tilted and in strain

Right: The easiest way of fixing the suspension spring (SS) to the suspension bracket (SB) is as shown here, where the suspension spring is held into a top block (TB) by simple pinning and then dropping into a suspension bracket saddle. This example is from a cheaply made lunar anniversary clock by Vosseler, c. 1910.

where it was fixed to the top block. The standard method, developed soon afterwards, was to fix the spring in a clamp (the top block), made of two halves screwed together and attached to a suspension bracket.

Some form of structure is needed to define the suspension bracket assembly on which the suspension spring assembly is to be hung. In form, the suspension bracket

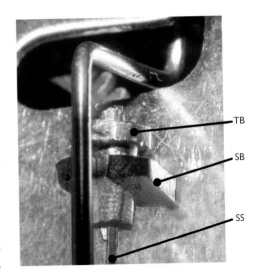

assembly consists of an L-shaped bracket mounted upside down, the short arm uppermost, and includes a second assembly for clamping and adjusting the suspension spring's top block. This second assembly, which may be nothing more than a hole in the bracket's short arm, has been broadly termed a 'saddle'. This term will used here to include any modifications to the short arm as well as any extra attachments, but to exclude the top block itself (note, however, particularly in the early clocks, the design of the top block can vary considerably).

Two issues arose with the early brackets. Firstly, the flat sides of a clamped suspension spring can swing from side to side without restraint, but as the wire strip is flat, no movement is possible from front to back. Secondly, as the clock has to be adjusted to put it in beat, freedom to rotate the top block is essential.

In this next development of the early Becker suspension brackets, not only can the suspension spring move freely from side to side but also from front to back, due to the pins added to the top block (TB). This removes the strain on the suspension spring during front-to-back movement while maintaining the vertical position. The top block rests in a separate, movable saddle part (S), which rotates for in-beat adjustment. (In the example shown a previous repairer has introduced a fault – the top block used is too deep, preventing free front-to-back swinging.)

Beyond the requirement of a stable point for hanging the suspension spring assembly, the supplementary requirements may therefore be summarised as:
(1) Free-swinging suspension spring movement in the front-back directions.
(2) Free rotation of the suspension spring assembly.
(3) Free provision to hang the suspension spring assembly on the suspension bracket without any dismantling being necessary.

The simplest way of fixing the suspension spring to a bracket would be some form of saddle into which the top block could be firmly clamped and which would provide no facility for moving or rotating the suspension spring assembly – in other words without (1) and (2). This, in fact, was the type of bracket offered with the early Becker and Vosseler clocks mentioned above. In this instance, placing the clock in beat required a permanent twist to be put in the suspension spring itself.

In Jfk's first production line of 1882, there was no provision for (1): the saddle is merely a hole in which a specially shaped top block, having a cylindrical lower portion, can be rotated. This was a style that dominated the early models (up to c. 1900) and also, via a slit in the saddle (added later), accommodated (3). Becker's and Jfk's were very similar, although Becker's has an extra clamping screw, which is usually missing because it interferes with (3).

Over the years there was a considerable number of small developments in the suspension bracket's saddle, culminating (in terms of complexity) in the Kienzle (1907) gimbals system (like a ship's sextant) and the final Becker (1906) system. In the gimbals-style saddle, full freedom for movement is offered in both directions with a top block that can be rotated in the innermost ring (as in early Jfk models).

In practice such involved ideas are not necessarily effective. For example: a clock is initially set up on a flat surface, but the customer is likely to have a surface that is out of true. The Kienzle gimbals system corrects automatically and fully for this; in the process, however, the original set-up position of the fork is altered. In-beat adjustments will therefore be affected, and this can contribute to an out-of-beat operation.

Below left: The first Jfk suspension bracket. The cylindrical part of the top block was screw-clamped into the suspension bracket. Loosening the screw allowed the suspension spring to be rotated for putting the clock in beat. (The suspension spring and fork have been removed for clarity; only the anchor pin (A) is visible.) Although the suspension spring has free movement from side to side, front-to-back movement leads to strain.

Below: Early top blocks, with the suspension spring (SS) screw-clamped between a block made up of two identical halves (left), were made with a cylinder-shaped lower portion. This style applied to the first Jfk and Becker anniversary clocks.

The need for a properly held suspension spring never disappeared but finally settled into various forms based on the original Badische method. The need to be able set up a truly vertical position of the anniversary clock on all surfaces was finally settled with two features: first (introduced in 1949 by Kundo), where a pointed or shaped tip was centralised in a 'guide cup' fixed to the base; these showed when the clock was level and also provided some protection against the pendulum accidentally smashing into the glass dome. Second (introduced by Kern and Sohne in 1951), adjustable balancing screws were added around the base. Kern and Sohne also patented a movable guide cup in 1953. The guide cup now had a secondary function: for travelling, the pendulum could be secured by raising the guide cup until the pendulum was locked against an added upper bracket.

These modifications, in one form or another, rapidly became standard, ending the suspension bracket problems in the process. After this date pendulum developments to the suspension bracket, and indeed mechanical anniversary clocks, tend to be cosmetic and degenerative.

ADJUSTMENT

The most important part of an anniversary clock, both in terms of its appeal and difficulty of adjustment, is the pendulum assembly. There are four fundamental questions relating to adjusting this assembly: how many pendulum rotations a minute should there be; how can the number of rotations per minute be adjusted; what size of rotation should the pendulum have; and how do you put the clock 'in beat'?

NUMBER OF ROTATIONS

The number of pendulum rotations required per minute for correct timekeeping is fixed by the gearing of the clock. Before 1914 eight rotations per minute was the standard.

Below right: This example shows the Haas method of allowing the suspension spring side-to-side and front-to-back movement without strain. For clarity, the top block is shown lifted from the saddle assembly, and the top block, suspension spring and fork are rotated 90 degrees anti-clockwise (seen from above). Note also that the saddle ring (SR) is pivoted between two pointed screws as opposed to the Becker pins which rest in a v-groove.

Far right: The Grivolas construction maintains the freedom of movement in a similar way to Becker but the construction is heavier. Shown here are the top block (TB), the saddle (S) on which the top block swings and which controls rotation for setting in beat, and the retaining arm (RA), which prevents accidental disassembly of the top block and saddle.

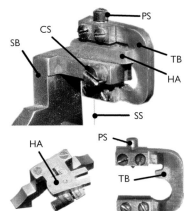

Above: The Badische version of the suspension bracket assembly. The top block (TB) hangs loosely on the large pin (P, left uncut for clarity) through the top of the saddle (S1), hence offering a simple, inexpensive method for the front-to-back movement. The saddle is friction push-fit into the top of the suspension bracket and can be rotated for putting in beat. S2, to the left of the illustration (seen from above and rotated 45 degrees anti-clockwise), shows the saddle attachment to the suspension bracket more clearly.

Above right: This popular Kienzle suspension bracket assembly appears on a number of makers' clocks. Clamped in the suspension bracket (SB) by a clamping screw (CS) is a holding arm (HA). The specially shaped top block (TB) hangs on the top of the suspension bracket with a pointed pivot screw (PS). The suspension spring (SS) is clamped to the bottom of the top block. Movement of the holding arm (for beat adjustment) rotates the top block. The whole assembly allows adjustable rotation for putting in beat, and free movement in both directions.

There are four methods of reducing the number of rotations per minute and thus making the clock go more slowly:

(1) To increase the weight of the pendulum.

(2) To re-distribute more of its weight to the periphery (without altering the total weight).

(3) To increase the length of the suspension spring.

(4) To make the suspension spring thinner, thus altering its stiffness.

To make the clock go faster the reverse of the above applies.

Method (1) is of interest because some of the later disc pendulums, such as Kienzle's, allowed coarse adjustment by the addition of thin discs inside the pendulum casing. Adjustment of the discs was normally the responsibility of the supplier, but other objects found, such as old coins (soldered in), are obviously user-added. Method (2) is satisfied by screwing the small adjustable weights outwards in the disc pendulum or adjusting the balls outwards on the ball pendulum. Direction of adjustment is usually indicated on a knurled disc at the top of the pendulum by the letter S (or F and S for 'fast' and 'slow'). A and R (*Avance et Retard*) appears on French clocks. This is the normal owner adjustment. Method (3) was used on the first non-adjustable pendulums (Badische) where an attachment effectively varied the length of the suspension spring. Methods (3) and (4) would be undertaken only by a repairer or restorer.

27

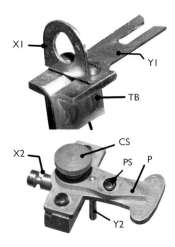

Above: In this 1907 example from Kienzle, the saddle consists of three rings. The outer ring is connected to the suspension bracket and is immovable. The middle ring of the three pivots on two screws mounted front and back, allowing free side-to-side movement. The inner ring pivots on two screws mounted at each side, allowing free front-to-back movement. The top block is mounted in the inner ring and may be rotated for setting in beat. The small screw in the side of the inner ring (visible in the illustration) is tightened when the clock is in beat.

Middle: This illustration shows the complicated Becker system (1906), which offers full freedom of movement, rotation of the suspension spring and no suspension spring bending strain. Part of the whole suspension bracket assembly is shown on the left of the illustration, explained in more detail below.

Upper right top: In the top block (TB) of the complicated Becker system, just the tip of the suspension spring is shown. The attached supplementary steel bracket has a hole at X1 and a fork at Y1.

Lower right: This shows the saddle, which is clamped to a flat, vertically mounted suspension bracket (SB). The hole at X1 swings freely on the saddle's stud, X2. The rod, Y2, constrains the rotational movement of the fork (Y1) and hence the pointer (P), for setting in beat. The pointer rotates about the pivot screw (PS), and is clamped after adjustment by the clamping screw (CS).

ROTATION SIZE

The pendulum rotates at the same rate whether linked to the clock mechanism or not. As the pendulum rotates, losses are mainly caused by friction. The mainspring power source, acting through the gear train and escapement, replaces losses via the pin on the anchor. The anchor pin acts on a fork attached to the suspension spring, which gives a push to the pendulum on each half-rotation or swing. The size of each pendulum swing either side of the pendulum's rest position is equal in a free pendulum (without anchor pin connected).

When the anchor pin is connected via the fork, the swing either side of rest varies according to the fork's datum position (varied by rotating the top block). The top block is rotated until each swing, either side of rest, is equal, hence putting the clock 'in beat'. The time taken for the pendulum to make one full rotation is approximately the same regardless of the size of the swing each side of rest (for quartz-like accuracy, wind the clock about every three months; mainspring force affects timekeeping slightly). The larger the swing the greater the power needed to keep the pendulum going and the poorer the accuracy. Too small a swing is to be associated with a poor escapement action. A complete pendulum rotation between three quarters and one full rotation would be correct for standard size movements.

Before starting any adjustments it is advisable to check that the number of revolutions per minute is correct. Remove the top block from the suspension bracket and re-assemble the other way round (so that the fork is disconnected and the pendulum rotates freely). Carefully turn the pendulum about three quarters of a turn and allow free rotation. Check for the correct number of turns per minute (eight per minute on early anniversary clocks). If there is any major deviation then the suspension spring will need changing.

Opposite left: One of the three adjustable balancing screws with its knurled edge protruding from inside the base. Also shown is the guide cup for levelling the base by centring the bottom tip of the pendulum – later ball shaped pendulums have allow for this. Right: The underside of the base, showing the fixing of one of the level adjusting discs (both in place and disassembled).

IN-BEAT ADJUSTMENT

It is important to recognise that operation on the top floor of a tall building is likely to be unreliable because of swaying. Likewise, operation near a railway line or heavy industrial plant can be unreliable, due to vibration.

Clocks are initially adjusted on a stable, level surface, and this condition must be maintained in subsequent use. If this is disregarded the clock will go out of beat and stop. For an anniversary clock to work reliably its pendulum must rotate an equal distance either side of the rest position. Adjustments to achieve this are known as putting the clock 'in beat'.

The easiest way to check for in beat is to observe the amount of rotation after a tooth drops (listen for the click on each rotation). First, rotate the top block until the clock is approximately in beat; next, adjust the height of the fork for a rotation between three quarters and one whole revolution; adjust the top block again as required. After each adjustment it will be necessary to allow the pendulum to settle down for some minutes before adjusting further. Leave running for at least half an hour before a final check.

Below: A complete pendulum assembly by Kienzle. The iron rings were added inside the pendulum to allow crude variations to the pendulum's weight.

CASEWORK
AND DISPLAY

THE PRIME requirement for all cases was that the pendulum had to be clearly visible while protected from air movement. For the more expensive clocks, the retailer would buy cases and movements separately, mixing them according to fashion and bespoke requirements. Among the heavily ornate and classical cases available, the brass, four-glass clock case, often plain, using bevelled glass and with access doors at the front and rear, has always been one of the most favoured. This last style of case was challenged, in terms of cost, by Badische and Kienzle. In their versions the four-glass assembly, using plain glass, lifted off like a dome. Both all-brass (Kienzle) and all-wood (Badische) frame versions were produced. It is possible the idea came from Becker, who as early as 1900 marketed an expensive version of the lift-off four-glass clock using silver-plated brass.

Opposite page: This lift-off four-glass case in brass is by Kienzle, c. 1910.

Left: An expensive, classical (French) four-glass case, embellished with onyx and made in the traditional manner; the movement used here is by Claude Grivolas (c.1910), and would have been matched to this case separately by the retailer.

Far left: This attractive mahogany case, with carved frontal motif, contains a standard anniversary clock mounted on a drawer, which slides out for winding and adjustment. It is dated c. 1930 and was by Kundo with a pendulum following the Kienzle style.

Top left: A lift-off four-glass case by Gustav Becker, c. 1900. The brass case is expensively made, silver-plated and with bevelled glass. The lever at the bottom of the case is slid along to lock the lift-off top.

Top middle: A second example of an anniversary clock by Claude Grivolas (c. 1910) but mounted in a more standard glass dome case. All the casework is oak.

Top right: A typical anniversary clock movement in an attractive wooden lanceolate-shaped case by Jfk, c. 1905.

Above left: An early-twentieth-century anniversary clock identifying display components: pediment spire finials (Ps), pediment (Pd), movement (M), dial (D), platform nut (PN), movement platform (MP), pillars (P).

Above middle: At the time this chrome-finished anniversary clock was produced (c.1930, Jfk), chrome was still a novelty, as was the Art Deco styling completed by an unusual pendulum style.

Above right: Dating from the first few years of the twentieth century, this example by Badische has a perfectly classical front but Badische's economies are apparent: the dial is plastic-covered paper and the pendulum (Kienzle) has a stamped-out gallery.

Below left: The first Jfk pediments were held at the top of the movement plate with the screws shown (Becker used a rear screw fixing). Note that the substantial pediment is as thick as the movement plate.

Below right: Badische's much thinner, flat pediment (c.1910) is stamped out and bent over. Spires are tapped and screw into the bent-over top of the pediment. The holes in the lower part of the pediment are used for attaching it to the movement.

On the everyday, price-conscious market, by far the most popular style of case was the one using a plain glass dome on a wooden or brass base; it is this style that has continued through to the present day with quartz movements, plastic domes, and even plastic bases.

Bottom: Four pediment spire styles. *From the left*: Becker, Badische, Jfk, Haas. In the earliest anniversary clocks the pillar nut holding the platform to the pillar assembly is a larger version of the pediment spires.

33

Top left: Dial and pediment style from Jfk, c. 1905.

Top middle: Square dial example of a popular Jfk pediment style.

Top right: This is one of the most popular pediment styles, appearing on Badische anniversary clocks.

Right: The classical origin of the pillar assembly is shown in this illustration. The column is also known as a 'pillar' or 'shaft'.

Below left: Two examples of movement platforms used to hold the movement to the pillar assembly. The first Jfk clocks used the right-hand style.

Below middle: Early pillar nuts are usually distinctive and specific to a manufacturer. This one is used almost exclusively on Haas clocks.

Below right: A standard, disassembled pillar system consisting of the column or pillar, capital (C), base (B), and pillar nut (PN). The pillar nut holds the movement platform to the pillar assembly via the clamping rod (CR). The lower end of the pillar rod is held below the clock's base with the washer and nut shown.

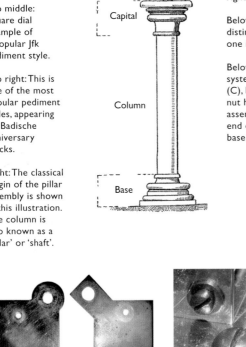

Capital

Column

Base

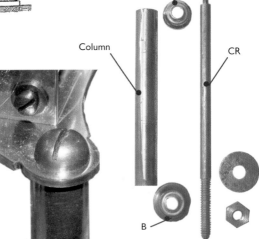

EARLY LUNAR
ANNIVERSARY CLOCKS

THE FACT that deGruyter allowed the patent for anniversary clocks to lapse in 1887 was either because they did not sell well enough or because the patent was too expensive to protect. Whatever the reason, the lapse of the patent appears to have led to a surge of competitive interest, and by 1900 the market situation had changed completely.

By about 1910 the market may still have been buoyant, but the competition to produce cheaper clocks was leading to a fall in quality. In all this Jfk adapted well and appear to have maintained a dominant position, attempting to undercut their competitors while expanding their range. In 1910 they manufactured a small round-plate movement, 60 cm in diameter, with cheap gears and no barrel round the mainspring. The movement was encased in a thin brass shell and had a two-ball pendulum, half the weight of a standard disc. The design required eleven pendulum rotations per minute.

The classical Greek *tholos* was an open, circular, pillared building with a domed top, the cupola. Clock cases based on this style are frequently seen with a French movement, strike and gravity pendulum. Especially large versions (38 cm high, with a dome diameter of 19 cm) had been made by Badische, Jfk and Haas using the standard 400-day movement, before the 30-day lunar anniversary clocks appeared in this style.

Jfk lunar anniversary clocks were made in two basic, though not unique, variants. One style followed the 400-day *tholos* form and was 33 cm (later 38 cm) in height with a dome 13.5 cm in diameter. The other was smaller in diameter (12.5 cm), with the movement mounted on a flat brass disc and positioned in place of the cupola. These clocks need to be wound monthly, hence the name 'lunar anniversary clock'. They are also known as 30-day clocks.

In 1910 Badische produced a 30-day movement. This was also a cheap mechanism but completely different from the one made by Jfk. In the rectangular-plate Badische version the movement and lightly textured plate surfaces were fully visible. In addition the Badische method of supporting the movement, by slotting the plates into the pillars, was unique. It was marketed in the standard 400-day glass-dome style with the standard

Similar in appearance to the Vosseler lunar anniversary clock (page 37), this *tholos*-style example is by Jfk. It is more substantially made with a good movement and enamelled dial.

The classic Jfk two-ball pendulum (c.1910) as used on all their lunar anniversary clocks. This is a well-made pendulum and is easy to adjust.

Badische three-ball pendulum (315 grams). In attempting to keep the price low, Badische used fewer gears, a pin pallet escapement (the type used in cheap wrist and pocket watches of the early twentieth century) and much thinner brass. The pendulum was required to have eight rotations in just under 65 seconds.

Some lunar anniversary clocks are mercury gilded: an amalgam of gold and mercury is painted on to the surface to be gilded. The surface is then heated to drive off the mercury. This process produces an excellent and attractive finish, but since mercury is poisonous, the technique is now illegal.

In 1910, Vosseler entered the market in competition with Jfk and Badische. A miniature round-plate 30-day movement very similar to that of Jfk was produced. At least six pendulums were offered: a two-ball pendulum, cheaply made, with balls mounted on a sprung loop and moved by an adjusting nut; two miniature three-ball pendulums, unique both in size and the crude method of construction; two miniature disc pendulums; and a standard-sized four-ball pendulum following the Kienzle style. All these were about half the weight of a standard 400-day pendulum. The size of the swing was smaller than in Jfk's model, and the movement was designed for ten rotations per minute.

The lunar anniversary clock movement as used in Jfk clocks. Note the pin-pallet escapement (A), the escape wheel (EW), and the hour wheel (HW).

Vosseler housed their movements in cases of at least three different styles. Two of the styles were very similar to the *tholos* style of Jfk. The third was a standard-sized glass-domed version similar to the one made by Badische but with the Vosseler standard-sized four-ball pendulum.

Vosseler offered their clocks with both solid pinion and the cheaper lantern pinion gears (the tall Jfk lunar anniversary clock used lantern pinions). With their solid pinion movements Vosseler offered good quality dials using painted numerals on a silvered surface and covered by a thin

brass sheet, which was breached over the numeral positions. Celluloid-covered paper dials were offered with the lantern pinion movements. Vosseler ceased production after 1914.

Badische used lantern pinions and celluloid-covered paper dials from the start, whereas Jfk started with lantern pinions and enamel dials but quickly adopted paper dials. Badische clocks sold well and are often to be seen at the antique shows – particularly their full-sized square-plate version. Jfk clocks, on the other hand, are relatively uncommon while Vosseler clocks are quite rare. In 1911 Kienzle produced a 30-day miniature clock with an unusual hemispherical pendulum. This is very rare.

A typical Jfk lunar anniversary clock with its unmistakable two-ball pendulum. This clock is not as well made as their *tholos*-style clocks. Note the plastic-covered paper face and the exposed copper plating on the brass. Originally the copper surface was mercury-gilded to prevent tarnish – a surface easily damaged by cleaning.

Far left: Movement of the inexpensive, very popular Badische full-size lunar anniversary clock. Note at the top, the pin-pallet escapement (common in most of the cheaper clocks of this period), the open mainspring, and lantern pinions.

Left: An example of a *tholos*-style lunar anniversary clock by Vosseler, c. 1910. The pillars are of blackened wood.

Bottom left: This rare example is a full-sized lunar anniversary clock by Vosseler (c.1910) and has a four-ball pendulum following the Kienzle style, but with a weight of about half that used in normal 400-day anniversary clocks.

Bottom middle: Rear view of the rare Vosseler lunar anniversary clock. As is customary with lunar anniversary clocks, the movement is enclosed completely and includes a push fit rear cap. The suspension spring extends through a hole in the lower part of the case.

Top left: The Vosseler miniature disc pendulum. Vosseler had quite a range of this style with varying degrees of ornamentation. They also made a small, primitive two-ball pendulum, a three-ball pendulum and a four-ball pendulum.

Top right: A labour-intensive Vosseler lunar pendulum. *Clockwise from top left*: Top view of the lunar pendulum; view from below showing that each ornament is laboriously screwed on and very accurately positioned in order to retain the balance (the centre rod fixing uses an hour wheel as a washer – the marks of the pincers used to hold and turn the circular nut are present but not visible here); the lid fitting beneath the pendulum; finally, the iron discs fitted in the body of the pendulum and used for coarse adjustment of the pendulum's weight.

Bottom right: This, the only other full-sized lunar anniversary clock, is by Badische and uses their standard three-ball pendulum. Again, the pendulum is about half the weight of a standard 400-day anniversary clock pendulum. In this unique and very popular clock, the mechanism is open.

FIRST ELECTRICS TO QUARTZ

THE FIRST electrical developments of the anniversary clock led to a standard mechanical anniversary clock with a normal-functioning torsion pendulum but a modified power source. The culmination of the electric phase, the quartz anniversary clock, was an entirely different development, which resulted in an electronic, printed-circuit 'movement' and a purely ornamental pendulum display; as such, an anniversary clock in appearance only.

THE FIRST ELECTRO-MECHANICAL CLOCKS

In 1945 August Schatz & Sohne was opened as the re-named descendant of Jahresuhren-fabrik. Where still mentioned on the clocks, the original Jahresuhren-fabrik became Jahresuhrenfabrik, while the back plate was also stamped with the month and year of manufacture. After 1953 clocks were stamped A., or Aug., or August Schatz & Sohne. The start of the 1950s saw Schatz's introduction of the all-mechanical miniature/midget plate sizes, such as the London Coach and the Bermuda Carriage anniversary clocks. The first electro-mechanical anniversary clocks appeared in *c.* 1956 based on this format. The first patent for a quartz crystal oscillator goes back to the 1920s (Cady), the era of valves (triode, 1908) and 19-inch rack mounting assemblies. In 1971, as transistorised quartz movements entered the scene, Schatz ceased manufacture of mechanical anniversary clocks, and only electrical versions were produced. By the end of 1986 the company had gone out of business and the

Bottom left: The Schatz Bermuda Carriage anniversary clock, 1956. Though not immediately apparent from the front, the deeper base allows space for a battery. Kern made a similar electrical mechanism.

Below: The base underside of the same clock. Note the adjustable levelling screws (1), the top cover release lever (2), battery negative terminal (3), battery positive terminal (4). Battery leakage is a typical problem, leading to the rust.

Right: An example
of the Schatz
electrical
remontoire
movement, c. 1956.
The coil is behind
the 7 on the dial.

Far right: Rear
view of the Schatz
electrical
anniversary clock.
Note the dating
stamp (October
1956).

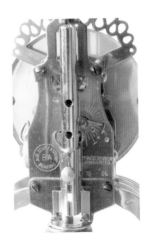

Schatz plant was razed to the ground; the termination, after a hundred years, of this famous company.

Previously, mechanical anniversary clock movements have been analysed in terms of power source, gear train, escapement and motion work. This breakdown is continued as the basis for the following.

POWER SOURCE

Below: A further
example of one of
the earliest Schatz
electrical
anniversary clocks
(c. 1956).

Mechanical anniversary clocks had used a wound mainspring; this was altered to a 'remontoire' type of system. Power was now produced by the rotation of a pivoted arm weighted at one end; in miniature form this is the equivalent of a weight-driven clock. The weighted arm gradually lowered as it drove the clock. At its lowest point the arm made contact with the armature of an electro-magnet. The armature of the electro-magnet now snapped shut while at the same time giving a sharp thrust to the weighted arm. The ratcheted, weighted end of the pivoted arm was swung upwards and held. This broke the armature contact removing power to the electro-magnet. The weighted arm now started to fall, powering the clock and repeating the cycle. These clocks only lasted on the market for a year or two and were claimed to suffer from contact difficulties. Problems exist because of the design of the electro-magnet's coil. In use, the battery and armature contacts must be kept very clean with a modern switch cleaner, and the battery should be replaced early. A small increase in battery voltage could be helpful, as could the addition of a capacitor across the battery. If (and only if) the user is fully experienced, soldering the leads between battery and holder, instead of using the clips, may lead to an improvement.

A 3-volt Ever Ready No. 8 Leclanche battery is situated beneath the base and is used to drive the electro-magnet. This battery is obsolete, though it can sometimes be sourced on the Internet. The No. 8 is also known as Energizer 2R10, Varta 3010, Vidor 004, Drydex 2T10, GEC BA6105, Oldham K809 and Siemens T8. Note that the chemistry is not the same as a modern battery, having a better shelf life and a different internal resistance. Two AA batteries in series or a re-chargeable 3-volt lithium battery are possible alternatives.

GEAR TRAIN, ESCAPEMENT AND MOTION WORK

With a mainspring, only a few turns are needed for winding fully. The gear train is necessary to convert these few turns to the many wheel rotations required at the escape wheel. The Schatz electro-magnetic anniversary clock uses only one intermediary gear to drive the escape wheel. The escapement and motion work are the same as those used in standard all-mechanical anniversary clocks.

QUARTZ ANNIVERSARY CLOCKS

The manufacture of electro-mechanical versions (also made by Kern – successor to Kienzle) only lasted a year or two. Transistorised quartz versions appeared in the early 1970s. The quartz movement was extremely cheap to produce, very accurate, and easily, safely and inexpensively transported in large quantities. It did not suffer from problems relating to temperature, or from levelling and beat problems, and its pendulum was now meaningless except as ornament. Unfortunately, attracting the cheapest of manufacture, cases were now mostly metal-sprayed plastic, very light in weight and with a tiny printed-circuit board 'movement'.

POWER SOURCE

Power was provided by a small, low-voltage dry battery accessed from the rear of the clock. This powered a small electronic circuit functioning both as an oscillator and drive unit for the motor. Again, the battery contacts must be kept clean.

GEAR TRAIN AND MOTION WORK

The electronic unit drives a small motor, which is connected to a plastic gear train driving the motion work.

ESCAPEMENT

Throughout the development of the anniversary clock – the most critical area – and the area receiving greatest attention – has been the oscillator (escapement and pendulum assembly). The remaining parts of the clock (power source and gear train) correct for power losses in the oscillator while also providing a visual

Above: Masquerading as an anniversary clock, this Westclox example belongs to the quartz era – some time after 1960.

Below: Rear view of the Westclox quartz anniversary clock with printed circuit boards removed. Note the plastic back cover with the shiny metal-sprayed finish.

Above: The front of the Westclox quartz anniversary clock movement removed from the clock. Note the battery terminals (1), the quartz crystal oscillator (2), and the white rod, which extends through the dial and to which the hands are fixed.

Below: Rear view of the wiring of the printed circuit board (3), as removed from the Westclox quartz anniversary clock. Note the wheel (1) for driving the suspension spring fork, the hand adjusting knob (2), the basic printed circuit board (3), and the miniature stepping motor (4) driven by the quartz oscillator.

record (motion work) of the passage of time. As the quartz oscillator forms the basis for modern clock manufacture, an explanation of its principles may be helpful here.

Consider a weight held above the ground. Before release it has a potential energy dependent on its height above ground level. On release the weight falls, faster and faster, until it hits the ground. Just before the moment of impact, the point of maximum velocity, all the potential energy has been converted into the energy of movement (kinetic energy). In a gravity pendulum clock, at the highest point just before the pendulum bob starts its fall (in an arc), the bob has maximum potential energy; note that this is relative to the lowest point reached by the bob (when the pendulum rod is vertical). At the lowest point, where the bob has maximum velocity, all the potential energy has been converted to kinetic energy, the energy of movement. Constrained by the pendulum rod, the bob continues to move until all the kinetic energy has been converted back to potential energy at the highest point on the other side of the swing; the process now repeats indefinitely, any losses being made up by the power source. This oscillation is the interchange between potential and kinetic energy under the influence of gravity.

Next consider the torsion pendulum as used in the anniversary clock. Oscillation is now the interchange between the kinetic energy (of the moving disc pendulum) and the potential energy stored in the twisting of the suspension spring. Gravity is no longer a controlling factor, being replaced by the stress in the twisting suspension spring.

In electrical circuits the components are less familiar but the oscillation process, between a coil and a capacitor, is essentially the same. A capacitor (condenser) is able to hold an electric charge or voltage (in the early days of electricity this was known as the potential difference — equivalent to the mechanical potential energy). The flow (electric current) of this charge through a conductor (or wire) constitutes the energy of movement similar to kinetic energy. A moving electric charge, an electric current, always produces a magnetic field. Winding a wire conductor into a coil allows the current to be temporarily 'stored', and at the same time the concentration produces a powerful magnetic field (useable, for example, as an electro-magnet). When the coil and capacitor are connected together there is an oscillation, or interchange, between the states of potential difference across the capacitor and the magnetic effect demonstrated by the current in the coil. The rate, or frequency, of this oscillation is decided by the physical characteristics of the coil and capacitor. The electronic oscillator circuit on a printed-circuit board automatically initiates the start of oscillation and makes up the losses (due to resistance or electronic friction). Quartz, as cut and shaped for electronic oscillators, is the equivalent of a coil and capacitor in parallel. Its advantage is that it is possible to cut the quartz to give a very low temperature co-efficient.

COLLECTING AND
THE WORKING CLOCK

A NNIVERSARY CLOCKS especially appeal to the collector who appreciates
the art in active mechanism and who enjoys the manipulative challenge
of their adjustment. In collecting, there are four aspects of particular interest:
case styles, unusual clocks, technical developments and simple restoration.

CASE STYLES

A display under a glass dome, so typical of the Victorian and Edwardian
periods, has always had a strong appeal. The skeleton
clock under a glass dome originated in the mid
eighteenth century. A skeleton clock is a normal
clock with a fully visible, skeletonised
movement – commonly with a standard
gravity pendulum but often with exotic and
very visual escapements. Extremely popular,
it was in vogue for over a hundred years, and
400-day versions were exhibited at the
Great Exhibition of 1851. However, by the
end of the nineteenth century skeleton
clocks were out of fashion.

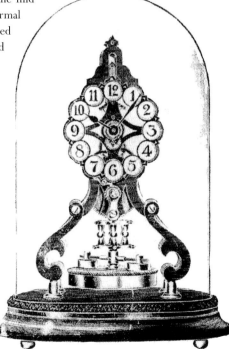

Right: This popular skeletonised anniversary
clock by Becker is shown here reproduced
from an original newspaper advertisement
(c.1905). It is shown with the Becker seven-
pillar, screwed-gallery pendulum (the seventh
pillar is central) with hook attachment for
the suspension spring. Becker pendulums are
immediately identified by the lower gallery
plate being of larger diameter than the
upper gallery plate.

A rare, sought-after design by Jfk, c. 1905, with top-screwed disc pendulum.

The mechanical anniversary clock therefore continued an established tradition. During the time it held the market the glass-domed version remained the most popular style and is still available (with quartz movements and plastic domes) in this form today. For the collector, the variations are enormous and reflect the changing artistic, social and economic conditions of the times.

Among the more ornate and expensive case styles the range was considerable, mostly with origins in the marble clocks and classical table clocks of the nineteenth century and before. However, the use of these ornate cases with anniversary clocks is invariably pre-1914 and particularly occurs with Jfk and Becker.

UNUSUAL CLOCKS

These include striking versions (Jfk and Schneckenburger), unusual escapements (Becker, Schneckenburger and possibly others), calendar displays (Kienzle and Petersen), skeletonised movements (Becker), examples by Grivolas (the only French manufacturer), rotating world and moon phases (Kaiser and Wurthner), 500- or 1000-day versions (Jfk under the Schatz badge), pre-1914 miniatures

This example of the Jfk London Coach model is mechanical. Together with the Bermuda Carriage model, it first appeared in the early 1950s. Both these models were used as the basis for the first Jfk electrical anniversary clocks. The immediate superficial difference may be seen in the extra base depth (to allow for a battery) of the electrical models.

(Jfk, Haas and Kienzle), large *tholos*-style versions (Jfk, Becker, Badische, Kundo and Haas), particularly ornate (Jfk) and Art Deco examples (Kundo), and low-production electro-magnetic clocks (Jfk and Kern). Clocks in all these categories are rare, the first three categories extremely so.

This early example anniversary clock by Kienzle (c.1910) has a wooden base, pillars in mahogany, and standard glass dome presentation.

TECHNICAL DEVELOPMENTS

With the exception of the motion work, movements tended to remain unchanged. Jfk, for example, used their 1882 movement, almost without modification, until the plate size became obsolescent in the 1950s, gradually giving way to smaller plate sizes and electro-mechanical movements. Cost cutting led to a reduction in the number of teeth on the gears of the motion work, and a high motion-work tooth count was the norm in marble clocks where movement of the minute hand is slightly less apparent. All the important mechanical technical developments are related to the pendulum assembly and mostly pre-date 1914.

RESTORATION

One would hardly collect anniversary clocks without hoping to have them

working, but there are major pitfalls. Many professional clockmakers refuse to work on them, and in the antique trade generally they have a reputation for inaccuracy, poor quality and the uneconomical nature of repair. Such complaints are based on the labour-intensive nature of both brass work cleaning and the intricate beat adjustment needed. Compared with any initial outlay, good professional restoration is therefore expensive.

An excellent and general practical background for repairing clock mechanisms will be found in de Carle's *Practical Clock Repairing* (*see* Further Reading). In addition to this, the following may be useful.

Left: A Badische anniversary clock using one of their most popular movements and their unique three-ball pendulum. Housed in the expensive four-glass case style, this model uses a lift-off wooden-frame case (stained oak), which makes accessibility simple while reducing the cost of production.

1. For cleaning brass, Brasso is the simplest and most laborious method. A motorised wheel using a loaded brush is ideal for tackling the worst brass surface. Alternatively, brass can be left to soak in special cleaners (see catalogues of Walsh, and Meadows & Passmore); for smaller parts an ultrasonic bath with special cleaner is very fast, but expensive.

2. Coating brass with a hot preservative (as at manufacture) can be emulated by heating the brass first with a hair-dryer. It is essential to wipe down thoroughly with methylated spirits. Transparent spray lacquers can be used, as can French polish, which can be diluted easily with meths.

3. Replacement suspension springs are available from the suppliers mentioned above. A pack containing the full range is usually essential. Slightly thinning a suspension spring is possible but it must be for the full length.

4. Standard forks, top blocks and bottom blocks are available from the suppliers. Missing top blocks for the older clocks may have to be fabricated by hand.

5. Correct setting in beat is critical. Before you make any adjustments, check that the clock is on a flat surface. With the fork disconnected check that the pendulum rotates approximately to the standard eight rotations per minute. Connect and roughly adjust the fork position for three quarters to one full rotation and adjust (rotate or equivalent) the top block to put the clock in beat (see chapter on pendulums). Allow time for the rotations to settle then correct the adjustments as necessary; fluttering may be removed by adjusting the fork position slightly. Allow the clock to run for half an hour to check the beat properly.

When the clock is running, as the escape wheel teeth move, a point is reached where a pallet suddenly drops. The pendulum movement should be equal after each pallet drop (both swings); if not the top block should be rotated to correct this.

As a rough guide only, and with the clock fully wound:

1. If the pendulum continues for about a quarter of a turn after a pallet tooth drops (i.e. one third of the movement in each swing is due to the momentum of the pendulum after receiving power from the impulse face of the tooth), and without any faults, the clock should go for the 400 days.

2. If the pendulum continues for more than a quarter of a turn after a tooth drops check for unstable timekeeping.

3. If the pendulum continues for less than an eighth of a turn after a tooth drops there is something wrong.

MAKERS AND
LOGOS

THE MAKER and date of a clock are most easily identified via the back plate. This is apparently simple when the maker's name or logo appears there; however, in many cases the name or logo seen is that of the retailer (who would have bought in bulk), while older clocks are most often unmarked. The most certain method of identification is therefore the position of the gear and screw holes as seen from the back plate. This can be compared against the listed variations in Terwilliger's *400-day Clock Repair Guide*, which lists over six hundred.

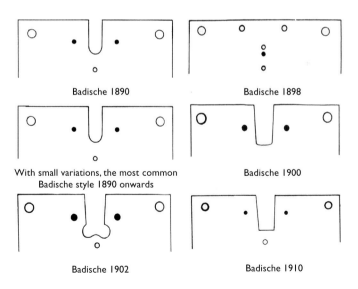

Badische 1890

Badische 1898

With small variations, the most common
Badische style 1890 onwards

Badische 1900

Badische 1902

Badische 1910

Badische Uhrenfabrik
Back plate suspension bracket cut-out variations

Unlike other manufacturers, Badische had a sequence of back plate changes due to different suspension brackets, pendulums and escapements. This illustration may be helpful in dating a Badische anniversary clock.

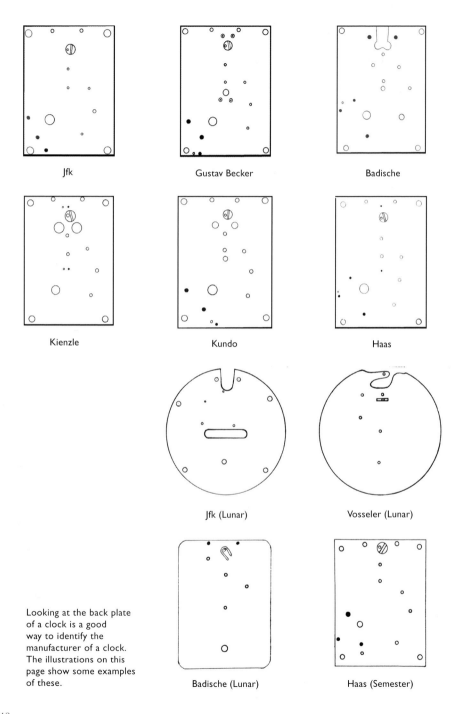

Jfk

Gustav Becker

Badische

Kienzle

Kundo

Haas

Jfk (Lunar)

Vosseler (Lunar)

Looking at the back plate
of a clock is a good
way to identify the
manufacturer of a clock.
The illustrations on this
page show some examples
of these.

Badische (Lunar)

Haas (Semester)

Many other defining features are contained within the text, and in addition, when a clock is stripped, a very valuable indicator is the number of wheel teeth (see illustrations) – this particularly applies to the motion work.

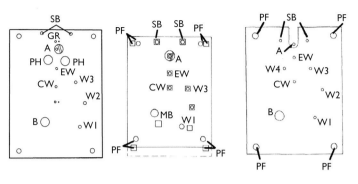

Left: In this example an extra wheel is present, W4, which immediately identifies the clock's manufacturer as Badische.

Top left: In this example, wheel positions (wheels 1–3, centre wheel, escape wheel and anchor) are shown by their first letter(s) and numbers. In addition positions are shown for the suspension bracket fixing (SB), peep holes (PH) for viewing the escapement during adjustment, and guard-ring fixing holes (GR) for the suspension spring guard. The guard-ring method of suspension spring protection immediately identifies the maker as Kienzle.

Top middle: In this back plate example the holes for a Jahresuhren-fabrik clock (round holes) have been superimposed on the square holes of a Becker clock (the Becker also has a slightly longer back plate). PF are the four pillar holes for fixing the plates, and MB is the main barrel.

Below: For the earliest clocks, one of the best but trickiest methods of finely identifying the maker and year of manufacture is to examine the wheel tooth count – particularly the motion work tooth count.

Year	Barrel	W1	W2	W3	Centre Wheel	Escape Wheel	W4	Minute Wheel	Hour Wheel	Cannon Pinion
1882		66/12	64/12	60/10				36/8	96	36
1884	86				96/8	20/8		36/7	84	36
1912		64/12	64/12	60/10				40/8	48	20
1952								40/12	48	16
c1899	84	70/12	62/12	64/10	96/8	20/8		32/6	72	32
c1910								30/8	32	10
c1890	80	60/10	54/9	54/9	45/9	12/9	36/9	36/10	40	12
c1902	64	60/8								
c1910	86	64/12	64/12	60/10	96/8	20/8		36/10	40	12

	1	2	3	4	5	6	7	8	9	10	11	12	13	14
	Maker	Ca	Spring	B	W1	W2	W3	CW	W4	EW	MW	H-CP	P'dlm	Weight
	Badische	1902	20/38	64	60/8	54/9	54/9	45/9	12/9	36/9	36/10	40/12	3B	250g
	Badische	1900	20/38	80	60/10	54/9	54/9	45/9	12/9	36/9	36/10	40/12	DG	338g
	Becker	1899	19/38	84	70/12	62/12	64/10	96/8		20/8	32/6	72/32	DSG	404g
	Becker	1910	19/38	84	70/12	62/12	64/10	96/8		20/8	30/8	32/10	DG	384g
	Haas	1904	19/36	86	70/12	60/12	64/10	96/8		20/8	36/7	84/36	3B	446g
	Haas	1905	19/36	86	70/12	60/12	64/10	96/8		20/8	36/10	40/12	DG	384g
	Haas	1905	19/36	86	70/12	60/12	64/10	96/8		20/8	36/10	40/12	DG	384g
	Henn	1952	19/38	86	84/12	64/12	62/10	96/8		20/8	30/8	32/10	4B/K	
	Jfk	1883	19/36	86	64/12	64/12	60/10	96/8		20/8	36/8	96/36	DNG	306g
	Jfk	1884	19/36	86	64/12	64/12	60/10	96/8		20/8	36/7	84/36	DNG	254g
	Jfk	1902	19/36	85	64/12	64/12	60/10	96/8		20/8	36/7	84/36	DSG	462g
	Jfk	1912	19/36	86	64/12	64/12	60/10	96/8		20/8	40/8	48/20	DG	422g
	Jfk	1952	19/36	86	64/12	64/12	60/10	96/8		20/8	48/12	48/16	4B/J	366g
	Jfk	1955	21/50	120	64/12	64/12	60/12	50/10	40/10	15/10	36/10	40/12	4B/J	146g
	Junghans	1910	19/36	86	64/12	64/12	60/10	96/8		20/8	36/10	40/12	2B/D	374g
	Kaiser	1951	19/38	88	82/10	78/10	48/9	48/9		20/8	36/10	40/12	W/EK	245g
	Kern	1951	19/36	90	64/12	64/12	60/10	96/8		20/8	30/8	32/10	4B/K	
	Kienzle	1910	18/36	86	64/12	64/12	60/10	96/8		20/8	36/7	84/36	DL	454g
	Koma	1950	20/38	96	64/12	64/12	60/10	96/8		20/8	36/10	40/12	4B/J	302g
	Kundo	1930	19/38	84	64/12	64/12	62/10	96/8		20/8	30/8	32/10	4B/K	238g
	W.W.	1953	19/38	86	64/12	64/12	60/10	96/8		20/8	48/12	48/16	4B/K	352g

(1) **Maker**; (2) Approximate Date of manufacture – **Ca**. (3) Mainspring (mm) – 1st Number = **Width of Spring**, 2nd Number = **Inside Diameter of Barrel**; (4) Number of Barrel teeth – **B**; (5) 1st wheel teeth – number of teeth on the wheel and pinion, smaller number is the pinion; (6) 2nd wheel teeth – as above; (7) 3rd wheel teeth – as above; (8) Centre Wheel teeth – **CW**, as above; (9) Badische 4th wheel teeth – **W4**, as above; (10) Escape Wheel teeth – **EW**, as above; (11) Minute Wheel teeth – **MW**, as above; (12) Hour Wheel and Cannon Pinion teeth – **H-CP**, hour wheel tooth count followed by the Cannon Pinion tooth count; (13) Pendulum type – **P'dlm**: **3B** = 3 ball, **DG** = top-screwed disk pendulum, **DSG** = screwed gallery disk pendulum, **4B/K** = Kienzle style 4-ball pendulum, **DNG** = Disk pendulum without gallery, **4B/J** = Jfk style 4-ball pendulum style, **2B/D** = 2-ball pendulum with integrated disk, **W/EK** = World pendulum, **DL** = disk pendulum with non-standard gallery; (14) Weight of pendulum in grams.

The following is a list of the better-known makers of mechanical anniversary clocks. The first year given is the date of market entry. Where a second date is given, it is the year when production ended but it indicates only the year when the company ceased to make key-wind (mechanical) anniversary clocks. A few companies continued with a developing range of electro-mechanical then electronic movements. As shown in the chapter on electric clocks these culminated in the modern examples (quartz) where the pendulum is pure ornament and has no effect on the timekeeping.

Badische Uhrenfabrik	1889 onwards
Gustav Becker	started (unsuccessfully) 1880; merged with Junghans 1926
Claude Grivolas	1908 to c. 1914
Phillipp Haas	c.1905–20
Sigfried Haller	c.1950–80
Edgar F. Henn	c.1953–54
Franz Hermle	c.1950–71
Uhrenfabrik Herr	1951–54 (bankrupt)
Ishisara Clock Company	c.1950
Jahresuhren-fabrik (Jfk)	1882–1971 (bankrupt 1985) (after 1945, August Schatz & Sohne)
Jauch and Haller	1948–c.1954
Gebruder Junghans	c.1910
Uhrenfabrik J. Kaiser	1954–62
Kern & Link	1929–32
Kern & Sohne	1937–86
Kieninger & Obergfell (Kundo)	c.1918–c.1980
Kienzle Clock Factories	c.1905–29 (sold out to Kern & Link)
J. Link & Co (formerly Kern & Link)	1952–57
Konrad Mauch (Koma)	1950–c.1980
Uhrenfabrik Neueck	1956–57
Nisshindo Watch Company	c.1965–73
Walter Petersen	1952–57
Uhrenfabrik M. Reiner	1961–65 (bankrupt)
Franz Vosseler	c.1908–c.1914
Georg Wurthner	1951–57

Many of the best-known makers' logos are shown in the following illustrations:

1. Phillipp Haas & Sohne
2. Badische Uhrenfabrik
3. Gustav Becker
4. Gustav Becker
5. Gustav Becker
6. Kieninger & Obergfell (K und O, or Kundo)
7. Junghans
8. Jfk
9. Schatz (using the JahresuhrenFabrik without a hyphen). Schatz rapidly introduced a replacement logo.
10. Jfk (using a hyphen, the original form)
11. Edgar F. Henn
12. Mauch Uhrenfabrik – Konrad Mauch (Koma)
13. Claude Grivolas
14. Kern & Sons

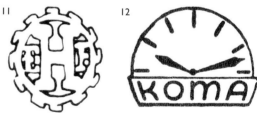

SUPPLIERS OF ANNIVERSARY CLOCKS

IT IS UNUSUAL to find many examples of mechanical anniversary clocks in collections in the United Kingdom. The best places to see a good range of these clocks and to gain hands-on experience and access to specialist knowledge, as well as an opportunity to purchase, are the major antique shows, clock fairs and horological specialists.

For antique fairs see *Antiques Info Magazine*, available quarterly. The two major fairs are at the Newark and Nottinghamshire Showground and at the South of England Showground at Ardingly, West Sussex. Major specialist clock fairs, the largest of which is held at Brunel University, Uxbridge, Middlesex, are advertised in *Clocks Magazine*.

Two major specialist sources for anniversary clocks are:

Olivers, 15 Cross Street, Hove, East Sussex BN3 1AJ.

Chris Wadge Clocks, 83 Fisherton Street, Salisbury, Wiltshire SP2 7ST.

Below right: An example of the popular skeletonised anniversary clock by Becker, with the same pendulum. In this coloured illustration, taken around a hundred years later, the time has been set to match that shown in the previously illustrated newspaper advertisement. This example, one of the most popular and expensive of the early glass dome (oval) anniversary clocks, appears not too infrequently on the antique market. For the highest price it should be with the matching skeleton pendulum shown to the right of the illustration – adjustable weights are held below the pendulum's body.

Far left: This early midget clock by Haas (c.1908) is in fact a 'semester' or six-month anniversary clock. This rare clock was found complete but in pieces and with a badly damaged base; it was therefore re-mounted on an attractive, old-style base. Note the combined disc and ball pendulum.

PLACES TO VISIT

GERMANY

Black Forest clock collections may be seen at the following museums:

Deutsches Museum, Museuminsel 1, Postfach 26 01 02, D-8000 Munich 22, Bavaria.

Heimat Museum, 7220 Schwenningen, Baden-Württemberg.

Heimat Museum, Wallfahrtstrasse 4, 7740 Triberg, Baden-Württemberg.

Heimatstuben, Scheuerlenstrasse 31, 3057 Neustadt, Baden-Württemberg.

Historische Uhrensammlung, Gerwigstrasse 11, 7743 Furtwangen, Baden-Württemberg.

Württemberg Museum, Altes Schloss, 7000 Stuttgart, Baden-Württemberg.

GREAT BRITAIN

Excellent clock collections can be seen at the following London museums:

British Museum, Great Russell Street, London WC1B 3DG. Telephone: 020 7323 8299. Website: www.britishmuseum.org.

Science Museum, Exhibition Road, South Kensington, London SW7 2DD. Telephone: 0870 870 4868. Website: www.sciencemuseum.org.

Victoria and Albert Museum, Cromwell Road, South Kensington, London SW7 2RL. Telephone: 020 7942 2000. Website: www.vam.ac.uk.

The Wallace Collection, Hertford House, Manchester Square, London W1U 3BN. Telephone: 0207 563 9500. Website: www.wallacecollection.org.

Right : After World War II Jahresuhren-fabrik was re-opened under the Schatz name to celebrate the company's founder. This example (October 1953), with the dome removed, was one of the last to be made with a standard-sized movement.

Far right: This example, showing a Badishe movement with their classic three-ball pendulum, is dated from the early years of the twentieth century. The pediment, extra movement wheel (or gear), lantern pinions and unique pendulum all define the maker.

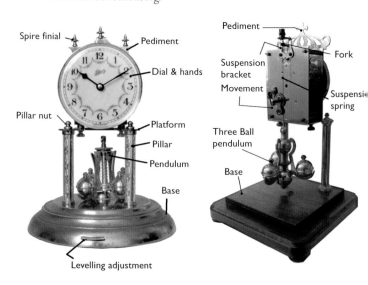

Spire finial — Pediment
Dial & hands
Pillar nut
Platform
Pillar
Pendulum
Base

Pediment
Fork
Suspension bracket
Movement
Suspension spring
Three Ball pendulum
Base

Levelling adjustment

FURTHER READING

de Carle, D. (1982) *Practical Clock Repairing*. NAG Press.

de Carle, D. (1983) *Watch and Clock Encyclopaedia*. NAG Press.

Kochman, K. (1992) *Clock and Watch Trademark Index*. Antique Clocks Publishing, Concord, USA.

Miles, M. (1989) 'Becker's Experimental Enigma' in *Clocks Magazine* 12 (5) p. 21.

Palmer, Brooks (1967) *Treasury of American Clocks*. Macmillan.

Penman, L. (1989) 'A Case for Your Anniversary' (two parts), *Clocks Magazine* 11 (11) pp. 47–51 and 11 (12) pp. 45–49.

Shenton, Alan and Rita (1996) *Collectable Clocks 1840–1940*. Antique Collectors' Club.

Terwilliger, C. (1991) *400-Day Clock Repair Guide*. Horolovar Company.

Terwilliger, C. (1983) 'The 400-Day Clock and its German Origins' in *Clocks Magazine* 6 (1) pp. 15–19.

Tyler, E. J. (1974) *Clocks and Watches*. Golden Press (Western Publishing Company Inc).

Wadge, C. (1983) 'Fault Finding Facts and Figures' in *Clocks Magazine* 6 (1) pp. 11–12, 40.

Wadge, C. (1983) 'Repairing a Kaiser' in *Clocks Magazine* 6 (1) pp. 20–22, 39–40.

Wadge, C. (1995) *The Hands-On 400-Day Clock Repair Guide*. Chris Wadge Clocks, Salisbury.

Wilford, A. (1995) 'Saunders of Sydney' in *Clocks Magazine* 17 (8) pp. 20–23.

Wotton, P. (1990) 'A Flutter on the Four Hundreds' in *Clocks Magazine* 13 (2) pp. 39–41.

Wotton, P. (1991) 'An Early Torsion Pendulum' in *Clocks Magazine* 14 (1) pp. 16–19.

Wotton, P. (1995) 'Anniversary Twins' in *Clocks Magazine* 17 (12) pp. 12–15.

Wotton, P. (1996) 'The Kienzle Copy' (two parts) in *Clocks Magazine* 19 (1) pp. 12–14 and 19 (2) pp. 41–43.

Wotton, P. (2003) 'Anniversary Brackets' (two parts) in *Clocks Magazine* 26 (2)

INDEX